IN THE OUTDOORS

SAFETY

K. Carter

The Rourke Press, Inc.
Vero Beach, Florida 32964

PHOTO CREDITS
© Emil Punter/Photovision: title page, p. 7, 12, 15; © Kyle Carter:
cover, p. 4, 13, 17, 18, 21; courtesy National Oceanic and
Atmospheric Administration: p. 8; courtesy National Severe Storms
Laboratory: p. 10

Library of Congress Cataloging-in-Publication Data

Carter, Kyle, 1949–
    In the outdoors / by Kyle Carter
        p. cm. — (Safety)
    Includes index
    ISBN 1-57103-079-4
    1. Outdoor recreation for children—Safety measures—Juvenile
literature. 2. Children's accidents—Prevention—Juvenile literature.
[1. Outdoor recreation—Safety. 2. Safety]
I. Title II. Series: Carter, Kyle. 1949-   Safety
GV191.625.C37   1994
796.5'028'9—dc20   94–12677
                                                     CIP
                                                     AC

Printed in the USA

TABLE OF CONTENTS

OUTDOOR SAFETY

Whenever you're outdoors, play it safe! Being safe in the outdoors means that you need to keep your wits about you. You need to prevent outdoor accidents before they happen.

Some of the most familiar places can be the most dangerous—if you're not careful. By being careful, you can keep yourself safe around streets and train tracks and in playgrounds, parks and woodlands.

A walk in the woods is great fun, but after your hike, check carefully for the presence of ticks

PLAYGROUNDS

Playground activities are fun and exciting. Playgrounds can be dangerous if you're not careful.

Wait your turn for playground equipment. Don't let friends talk you into using equipment that is too difficult for you. Climb and swing only at heights where you are comfortable.

Be especially watchful of moving objects—swings, baseball bats, seesaws and merry-go-rounds.

When you're not on a swing, keep a safe distance away

TORNADOES

A sky that begins to darken usually means that a **severe**, or harsh, storm is near. Severe storms bring thunder, lightning and sometimes **tornadoes**.

A tornado is a whirling, funnel-shaped cloud. If the tornado touches down, its powerful winds cause horrible damage.

If you are outdoors and see a tornado, run to a ditch or basement for safety.

A tornado's funnel-shaped cloud is a powerful, whirling storm

ELECTRIC STORMS

Thunder is loud, but harmless. A streak of lightning, though, is actually a bolt of electricity. A lightning bolt that snakes to the ground can kill.

The best way to **avoid** being struck by lightning is to go quickly into a car or house. If you cannot take shelter indoors, remain low to the ground. Stay away from tall trees and water.

The use of sun block will help prevent sunburn and serious skin diseases later in life

Watch alligators and other wild animals from a safe and respectful distance

STOP, LOOK AND LISTEN

Streets were made for cars and trucks. Streets are safe for people walking only when the cars and trucks have passed.

Stop, look and listen before crossing a street. If you are standing by a traffic light, look for the "walk" signal before you begin to cross. Do not step off the curb until the street is clear. Never play in the street.

If a ball or pet goes from your yard into the street, do not run into the street after it.

Never chase a ball into the street until you stop, look and listen for traffic

TRAINS

Do not play around train tracks. Trains often move at faster speeds than cars. A train can be upon you much faster than you might expect.

Never cross railroad tracks without stopping, looking and listening. If one train passes, make sure that another train is not approaching on the next track.

Help people on the train keep safe, too. Never place objects on train tracks.

Never play on or near railroad tracks

CAMPING

One of the greatest safety **risks** when you are camping is the campfire. Be sure the fire is contained in a pit or in a circle of stones. Never leave the fire without someone to watch it.

Do not ever run or play near a campfire. If you trip, you can fall into the fire and be badly burned.

Keep a safe distance from campfires and never leave them unguarded

PLANTS

Most wild plants are harmless. Some are even good to eat. A few common wild plants, such as poison oak and poison ivy, cause rashes and itching.

Some kinds of wild mushrooms are good to eat. Others are poisonous. They cause illness or even death. Mushrooms are hard to tell apart. The best rule is to never pick and eat *any* wild mushroom.

Learn the harmful plants in your area and avoid them.

Learn to know the dangerous plants in your area, like the poison ivy shown here

ANIMALS

Any animal can be dangerous under certain conditions. You should never approach a wild or strange animal.

Beware of any wild animal that approaches you. A wild animal that shows no fear of people may have **rabies**. Rabies is a serious disease that an animal can pass on to people through a bite. The animals that may commonly have rabies are dogs, raccoons, skunks and bats.

Glossary

avoid (uh VOID) — to stay away from

rabies (RAY beez) — a serious, sometimes deadly disease usually spread through the bite of an animal with the disease

risk (RIHSK) — the chance of danger

severe (seh VEER) — harsh

tornado (tor NAY do) — a powerful, whirling windstorm that can cause severe damage

INDEX